THE WORDS OF THE BIBLE

2

PSALMS
OF
TRUST

St Paul Publications
The Liturgical Press

PSALMS OF TRUST
Original title: *I salmi della fiducia*
© 1988 Figlie di San Paolo, Milan, Italy

English language edition first published in June, 1991

Translated by Marie Therese Levey RSJ

Australian edition:
© St Paul Publications, 60-70 Broughton Rd, Homebush 2140
National Library of Australia
Card Number and ISBN 0 949080 15 2

United Kingdom edition:
© St Paul Publications, Middlegreen, Slough SL3 6BT
ISBN 085439 362 5

North American edition:
© The Liturgical Press, Collegeville, Minnesota 56321
ISBN 0-8146-1990-8

Typeset by the Society of St Paul, Wantirna Sth, Australia
Printed by Singapore National Printers, Singapore

CONTENTS

FOREWORD

The psalms constitute a universal heritage of poetry, unique and distinct; they are a constant reference for literature, but above all, for prayer — liturgical, personal and communal — and not only for the people of Israel in ancient times, but also for us, the church of today, the people of the new covenant.

All the combined wealth of attitudes and sentiments of a humanity which painfully suffers — silently enjoys or rejoices — seeks and loves God — meditates — petitions — or give thanks and praises — is contained in the 150 psalms. There is not one person who can remain untouched by the prayers in these psalms, such is the strength, truth and authenticity of expression in them.

Each of us can see ourselves reflected in them, and that is why we can consider the prayer of the psalms as our own personal prayer.

In this booklet are collected some 'psalms of trust' upon which we can reflect and, in turn, pray. Indeed, these psalms awaken hope in us, and invite us to place all our trust in the fidelity of God.

After each psalm (of which either the whole or a selected passage is presented), there follows a short meditation and thought, intended to help us understand the particular subject in the passage and to make its meaning more realistic in our daily life.

The Publishers

THE INFINITE ONE WAITS FOR ME

Faith and trust support people on their journey of life. The Hebrews needed faith and trust to be able to dream, to wish, and eventually, to reach the Promised Land.

Through the ages it has always been the same and for each one of us today the reality remains.

To have faith is to see beyond appearances — to strive for, and to want to see the infinite, even when the appearances are such that they could make themselves felt as the reality, and so seem to make the earthly enjoyment sufficient without thought of the eternal enjoyment awaiting those who truly trust God. To have trust, then, is to be able to say to God, 'I love you', and through the love of the Creator in return, be able to love all creation, recognising each person and every part of it as God's great masterpiece.

To have trust means to search constantly for ways of making this harmony in creation go beyond appearances and beyond so many stubborn 'I's', who claim for themselves everything except God.

Trust is to walk above the appearance, so that realities, even though they are invisible, may become daily bread for each one: a bread that humanises the cosmos — all of it — even the hardest stones, which can also be gifts from God.

To have trust is to believe God is near, even if the sky is dark and the horizon is distant.

Each ray of light, however small it may be, contains hope. Beyond the clouds, even though they be dense and dark, there is a God who has longings for us, thoughts of us, wishes for us, and in infinite love, waits for us.

Meanwhile, we try, in trust, to catch a glimpse of this God.

And, why not?

Giorgio De Capitani

**MY REFUGE
AND MY STRENGTH
MY GOD IN WHOM I TRUST**

TRUST IN GOD OUR SAVIOUR

from Psalm 108

O God, my heart is steadfast,
I will sing and make music, with all my soul.
Awake, lute and harp! I will awaken the dawn.

I will thank you, O Yahweh, with the peoples;
I will sing your praise with the nations;
for your mercy is higher than the heavens,
and your faithful love reaches the skies.

Be exalted, God, above the heavens,
your glory far above the earth.
Save by your might and answer me,
that those you love may be delivered.

Who will lead me to the fortified city?
who will guide me into Edom?
Only you, who have rejected us.
You march no more, O God, with our ranks.

Grant us help against the foe;
for human help is vain.
Through God we shall fight courageously,
for God will trample down our foes.

The living God, who is the saviour of all people (cf. 1 Tim 4:10), has sent Jesus as the unique redeemer of the world. In no one else's name can we be saved (cf. Acts 4:12). To God's goodness, therefore, goes all our praise; in God is all our trust and the fullness of our gratitude, sure as we are in the promise of justice and liberation.

The first ray of light
is a prayer of praise by all creation,
and our first yawn in the morning
can be an act of thanks for life,
and thanksgiving also for
the loved house of God ...

TRUST ON THE WAY

from Psalm 91

Whoever dwells near the Most High's walls,
will live in the Almighty's shade.
I will say to Yahweh:
'My refuge and fortress,
my God whom I trust.'

A thousand may fall at your side,
ten thousand to your right,
but you will be unscathed.
You have only to look to see
the payment received by the wicked.

If you make Yahweh your safe retreat,
the Most-High your dwelling place,
no disaster shall come on you,
no misfortune approach your tent.

The Most-High will put angels in charge of you,
to guard you wherever you go.
They will hold you up in their arms,
so your feet are not injured by stones.
You can tread on the lion and the adder;
you can trample on the lion and the snakes.

'I will save them because they are faithful to me;
I will raise them because they trust in my name.
When they call to me, I will answer them;
in times of trouble I shall be with them;
I will rescue and honour them.

'With long life I will satisfy them.'

'Strangers and exiles on the earth' (Heb 11:13).

Each day we travel part of our journey, trying to give meaning to the precious time which is passing. It is in the present, in the daily grind, that we extend God's reign, which is already amongst us, but not yet completely (cf. Lk 17:21). It is the Lord who answers our prayer, thus helping us to continue and complete the work of creation.

Under your great wings, O God,
I feel secure;
your angels will support
my tired steps,
and the stones — any stone —
obstacle or doubt,
will not cause me to stumble any more.
I will even be able to walk on my own
through deserts.
You will save me
and answer me when you see my eyes
turned towards you.

TRUST WHEN IN DISTRESS

from Psalm 7

O Yahweh my God, in you I find refuge.
Deliver and save me from all who harass me,
lest they tear at my throat like a lion with prey,
and drag me away with no one to rescue.

Let Yahweh judge the peoples;
judge me, O Yahweh,
as my innocence merits
and my inner integrity.

O God of all righteousness,
searcher of hearts and minds,
stamp out the wicked;
grant strength to the just.

My shield is God Most High
who saves those who obey.

I will raise thanks to Yahweh
because of God's justice,
and sing to the name of Yahweh Most High.

Jesus experienced anguish (cf. Lk 22:44; Mk 14:36) and prayed to God to be freed from it. Jesus was the innocent one and that innocence enables us, when suffering, to go with confidence to that one who knows what suffering means.
We will not be abandoned, for our life is precious in God's eyes.

God, you will always look with kindness
on those whose hearts are just.
You judge with justice
so why need I be afraid?
Sinners dig their own pit of evil
and bring upon themselves their just desserts;
keep me in your love,
then I need never be afraid of your justice.

TRUST AND ABANDONMENT IN THE LORD

from Psalm 11

In Yahweh I take refuge.
How can you say to me,
'Flee like a bird to the hills?

'See how the wicked bend their bows,
their arrows ready upon the string,
to shoot at the upright from shadows.
When foundations are destroyed,
what can the righteous do?'

Yahweh is in the holy Temple;
Yahweh has set firm the heavenly throne.
God's eye is on the human race;
taking its measure at a glance.

Yahweh tests both just and wicked;
hating all those devoted to violence.
Yahweh showers the wicked with fire
and sulphur;
a scorching wind is their reward.

Yahweh is righteous, devoted to justice,
Yahweh's face looks with favour on the just.

'Father, into your hands I commit my spirit' (Lk 23:46). These were the final words of Jesus who had come amongst us to fulfil God's will (cf. Mt 26:39). Amidst the crowd, God looks for each one of us, waiting with infinite patience — infinite because of God's divinity — to show and share with us the friendship already realised in Jesus.

My home is in you, God,
and when you say
'fly like a sparrow towards the mountain'
I know it is to you I am winging.

THE TRUSTFUL PRAYER OF A PEOPLE

from Psalm 60

You have cast us off, O God, and broken us.
You have been angry; take us back.

You shook the land and split it open;
bind up the rifts, for it trembles still.
You have made your people drink
a bitter draught;
you have given us wine that makes us drunk.

You have raised a banner for those who fear you,
a rallying point beyond range of the bow,
so that they may be saved who are dear to you,
Save us and help us with your right hand!

Grant us help against the foe;
for human help is vain.
Through God we shall fight courageously,
for the Lord will trample down our foes.

The assurance '... none who put their trust in God will lack strength' (1 Mac 2:61) and the promise, '... it is the Lord your God who goes with you' (Deut 31:6) are guarantees of success. Every day is a step towards tomorrow, when God will dry every tear, and transform every oppression into freedom.

Your people, O God,
weep bitter tears;
our faces are sad like those of exiles in flight;
you cause the earth to quake
while the cannons send out fires like those of hell —
Shall we live to see a new dawn?
Behold — a gleam of light!

PRAYER FOR HELP

from Psalm 140

Save me, O Yahweh, from evildoers;
keep me out of the way of the violent,
whose hearts are bent on evil schemes,
who spend their days provoking wars.

Their tongues are sharp as serpents' fangs;
vipers' venom is under their lips.
Keep me, O Yahweh, from wicked hands;
protect me from the violent mob
who try to thrust me out of the way.

I said, 'O Yahweh, you are my God.'
Listen, O Yahweh, to my prayers.
O Yahweh, God, my saving strength,
you shield my head when battle comes.

I know that Yahweh secures justice to the poor
and makes common cause with the needy.
Surely the just will praise your name;
the honest will live in your sight.

'The Lord will rescue me from every evil and save me ...' (2 Tim 4:18). This is the certainty upon which is based every choice in the lives of believers. We '... have been set free from sin and have become slaves of God' (Rom 6:22). If God takes our part, of whom should we be afraid? With Christ, who was unjustly persecuted — and with all the victims of persecution, torture, war, and every sort of violence — we ask God trustfully, as friends, for forgiveness, freedom and justice.

It does not matter to me
if I should stumble
because of another's deceptions;
what matters is
that I still believe in that person —
and pity the human weakness —
after all, who am I?
You, O God, are humanity which loves,
you are humanity which hopes,
you are humanity on the journey — forgive me
that I cannot love — as you love.

I LIFT UP MY VOICE
TO THE LORD
WHO ANSWERS ME

THE HYMN OF THE ONE BLESSED BY THE LORD

from Psalm 116

My trust did not fail even as I said,
I am bitterly distressed.
In my terror I cried,
'All people are faithless'.

How can I repay all that Yahweh does,
for all the gifts poured on me?
I will lift up the cup of salvation
to call on the name of Yahweh;

and pay my vows to Yahweh
in the face of God's people.
A precious thing in Yahweh's sight
is the death of those who die faithful
to the Most High.

Truly, O Yahweh, I am your slave;
I am your slave,
the child of your slave.
You have loosed the fetters that bound me.
To you I will bring a gift of thanksgiving,
and invoke Yahweh by name.

I will pay my vows to Yahweh
in the face of all the people,
in the courts of Yahweh's house,
in the midst of you, Jerusalem.

Jesus — our Emmanuel, God amongst us, one of us — remains with us in the Eucharist (cf. Jn 6:51). Jesus is present also in the person I so often judge severely. It is the Lord who brightens spirits and restores peace, and for this, we, who are so blessed by God, express deep gratitude. In fact, the Lord always offers us the opportunity to be victorious in Christ, even when everything appears dark in life (cf. 1 Jn 5:4).

I thank you today, Lord,
in the strong hope
that my present freedom
from the snares of the deceitful
(who have besieged my soul
with golden chains),
will continue.
Lord, look on my cup;
your silent watch is enough for me.

I CALL TO GOD WHO RENDERS JUSTICE

from Psalm 54

Save me, O God, by your name;
set me free by your might.
Listen, O God, to my prayer;
hear me as I speak to you.

The violent are attacking me;
pitiless people seek my life.
They give no thought to God.
surely, my defence is God:
Yahweh, mainstay of my life.

I will freely sacrifice
to praise you, O Yahweh,
as is right.
For you have saved me from all troubles.
I watch with delight as my enemies fall.

The Lord renders justice to the poor and defends them. Jesus is our saviour, but also a just judge (cf. 2 Tim 4:8). In the same way, Christians try to walk together with their brothers and sisters in this world, contributing to the building of truth into love (cf. Eph 4:15).

As soon as I invoke you
I hear your voice, O God,
and nothing will be able to ruffle my faith,
which then becomes an act of love.

PRAYER OF THE JUST ONE

from Psalm 17

O Yahweh, hear my righteous plea;
pay attention to my cry;
hear my prayer
— it is not from lying lips.

May my vindication come from you;
may your eyes see what is right.
You probed and watched me all night long;
your tests have proved me innocent.

I have resolved that my mouth will not sin.
As for human deeds,
guided by your spoken word,
I avoided the path the violent tread.
My steps stay firmly on your way;
my feet secure, I never slip.

O God, I call; you answer me.
Listen to me; hear my words.
Prove to me your faithful love,
you who save by your right hand
all who seek you when attacked.

Guard me as the apple of your eye;
hide me in the shade of your wings,
from the wicked who attack me,
as deadly foes close in on me.

But my plea is just; I shall see your face;
my blessing will be seeing you when I awake.

*J*esus the Master speaks: 'Let not your hearts be troubled; believe in God, believe also in me' (cf. Jn 14:1). In Christ we can feel ourselves free and calm, and we are at the stage of overcoming every fear and anxiety brought about through human misunderstanding. It is Jesus who can touch the hearts, the mouths, and the feet of each one of us, so that our thoughts, words and actions become filled with God's Spirit.

**At times the sweetness of
God's response —**
like a whisper, a cry, or the voice of a child —
is of great comfort to me.
You care for me, Lord,
as the apple of your eye;
you protect me in the shadow of your wings;
you remember today
every person who is poor and alone;
and you are mindful of my concerns
for a better tomorrow.

MORNING PRAYER

from Psalm 5

O Yahweh, hear my words,
consider my sighing;
listen to my cry for help,
my King and my God
for to you I pray.

By morning, O Yahweh, you hear my voice;
by morning, I put my case to you,
and I wait.
You are not a God
who takes pleasure in evil;
no wicked can ever be your guest.
The proud will not stand your eyes.

But your faithful love is so great
that I may enter your house,
and bow down in awe
at your holy temple.

But let all who make you their refuge rejoice,
let them sing with joy forever.
Shelter those who love your name;
they rejoice in you.

For you, O Yahweh, will bless the righteous;
your favour surrounds them like a shield.

*Our lives, since their dawning,
have opened themselves to God,
waiting, in order to walk during the
day as children of the light. We
strive to do our utmost, searching
for what is pleasing to God
(cf. Eph 5:8-10), in order to build,
in daily encounters, the blessed
hope (cf. Tit 2:13) to which we are
called, and to which we aspire from
the depths of our beings.*

At the first sounds of a new day
my waiting heart stirs
and I think of you, O Lord;
and I think of the evil
which will occur today;
is it just another day which will pass
without meaning?
In you, Lord,
we find fresh hope in the new dawning of light.

GOD IS THE DEFENCE
OF THOSE WHO SUFFER

from Psalm 3

My foes are many, O Yahweh;
many there are who rise up against me,
many who say of me,
'God will not save that person.'

But you are the shield at my side, O Yahweh;
my glory, you hold my head up high.
Whenever I cry
Yahweh answers me from the holy hill.

I lie down to sleep,
and I wake up again,
for Yahweh upholds me.
I do not fear forces in thousands and thousands
drawn up against me on every side.
Arise, O Yahweh, save me, my God!

You strike all my foes across the face;
you break the teeth of the wicked ones.
From Yahweh comes deliverance.
May you bless your people.

What suffering occurs in the secret depths of each person, and what sorrow we have all witnessed in each other! In the search for relief and peace, we come face to face with God who is the Good Samaritan (cf. Lk 10:26-37), our unique and true refuge (cf. Ps 7:1) and the friend who supports us.

At each dawn I cry to you, Lord,
to give peace to those who suffer
because of the ceaseless urgings
of violence and sorrow;
the first sunray of each morning
opens my heart to you.

PRAYER OF THE JUST ONE BETRAYED

from Psalm 55

Hear my prayer, O God,
do not ignore my plea.
Hear me and answer me.

My cares leave me no peace;
I am quaking at the hostile shouts,
at the clamour of the wicked,
who heap up trouble against me
and revile me in their fury.

I call to God
and Yahweh will save me.
At dusk, dawn and noon
I cry out in distress,
and Yahweh listens to me.

God ransoms me and gives me peace
from the strife against me,
though many oppose me.
God, enthroned in eternity,
will hear them and strike them,
who never change, never fear God.

On Yahweh cast your cares;
and you will be sustained.
God never lets the just fall.

'Ask and it will be given you;'
(Mt 7:7). Jesus teaches that no
prayer is in vain, and invites us to
pray without becoming too tired
(cf. Lk 18:1-8). Jesus enlightens us
how to pray authentically to God
(cf. Mt 6:5-15) and faithfully
intercedes for us (cf. Rom 8:34).

Give me peace, Lord,
morning, noon and evening,
and on every part of the road;
wickedness is violent like a
surging sand storm.
On you I will throw my distress, O God,
and in you I will rest.

PRAYER OF THE ELDERLY PERSON

from Psalm 71

I will come and declare your mighty acts,
O Lord of all,
and proclaim your justice, yours alone.
O God, you have taught me from my youth;
all my life I have told of your mighty acts.

Even when I am old and grey,
do not desert me, O God,
until I have told of your strength
to generations still to come,
your might to all who are still to come.

Your righteousness reaches the skies, O God;
you have done such great things;
who is like you?

You have shown me troubles,
many and bitter,
but you will restore my life again;
you will raise me again from the depths of earth.
Restore me to honour;
give me comfort again.

I will praise you on the harp,
for your constancy, O God;
I will praise you with the lyre,
O Holy One of Israel.
My lips shout for joy as I sing to you,
for you have redeemed me.
All day long my tongue tells
of your just deeds.

'Anxiety brings on old age too soon' (Sir 30:24), but the just who confide in the Lord will bear fruit in their advanced years. Hope preserves youth in persons, and assists them to renew themselves continually in mind, so that they may discern what is good and wholesome to the Lord (cf. Rom 12:2).

You are my hope, O God!
You have always been that;
my support ever since I was young;
and during many years
you have enabled my faith
to resist endless temptations.
With the passing of time
your love for me has not lessened,
even when I let human miseries
weigh upon my heart;
from the time I was a baby
at my mother's breast
until today
I have learned just things from you.
I proclaim your wonders, O my God.

PRAISE OF THE FAITHFUL FRIEND OF GOD

from Psalm 112

Blessed the one who fears Yahweh,
who finds delight in God's commands.
The children will be great in the land,
an upright race forever blessed.

The house will be full of blessings and wealth,
where justice endures forever.
Even in darkness light shines for the upright,
for the gracious, compassionate and good.

Good comes to one who is gracious in lending,
whose business is managed with justice.
Surely such will never be shaken,
remembered forever for justice.

Bad news will bring no fear
to a steadfast heart that trusts Yahweh.
A steadfast heart need never fear,
for all things end in triumph over foes.

The poor who gain from lavish gifts,
bring good renown that never fades,
and dignity held high in honour.

Just persons are those who trust God and call themselves children of the Lord (cf. Wis 2:13). Such people receive in exchange everything that is good (cf. Lk 11:9-13) and above all, the Holy Spirit; and, as well, the capacity to love, to give of oneself, and to forgive others. The just are made worthy to receive the gospel (cf. 1 Thess 2:4), to preach it, and to allow themselves to be transformed from the gospel's teaching.

Those who love you, O God,
are just
and their works are just;
such people are never selfish,
but at all times are friends with the needy;
— O my God — how little I love you!

**LORD, LET YOUR GRACE
BE UPON ME
IN YOU I TRUST**

PRAISE TO THE PROVIDENCE OF GOD

from Psalm 33

That nation is blessed whose God is Yahweh,
the people chosen to be God's own.
Yahweh looks down from heaven,
and sees all the peoples of the earth.

From heaven Yahweh watches
all who live on earth.
God it is who fashions all hearts
and keeps a watch on all they do.

But Yahweh's eyes are on those
who fear the Lord,
on those who trust in Yahweh's faithful love
to save them from death
and preserve them in famine.

We are waiting for Yahweh,
our help and our shield,
and our hearts rejoice in the One
whose holy name we trust.

Yahweh, let your faithful love
rest on us,
as we have put our hope in you.

God loves the world and the creatures who live in it, watching over their waking and their sleeping, and foreseeing all their needs. We know what tiny creatures we are, so why do we trust in ourselves (cf. 2 Cor 1:9)? It is better to trust in the loving providence of God, to whom we are, indeed, more precious than the sparrows, and more important than the flowers of the field (cf. Lk 12:6-7).

Our hearts express
deep-felt cries that are ever new,
to the One who creates
horizons of peace and light bringing warmth;
God looks on us from on high,
— searching us from within —
and seeing us all,
the good as well as the wilful;
God, whose precious possessions we are,
keeps vigil at night
while we rest securely in hope.

TO THE GOD OF PEACE

from Psalm 144

Blessed be Yahweh, my rock,
who trains my hands for war,
my fingers for the fight.

Yahweh is my faithful love, my fortress,
my stronghold and my saviour,
my shield, my place of refuge,
who subdues nations under me.

O Yahweh, what are humans
that you should show them care?
What are frail mortals
that you spare them a thought?
They are like a breath,
their days but fleeting shadows.

Stretch down your hand from above,
deliver me and rescue me
from mighty seas and aliens' hands.

I will sing you a new song, O God,
songs to the sound of a ten-stringed lyre,
to the One who gives victory to rulers,
and rescue to David, your servant,
from the deadly sword.

*J*esus has conquered the world
(cf. Jn 16:33) by assuming every
type of evil: violence, oppression
and injustice — and any other evils
that have roots in the human heart,
where such evil is sin. In infinite
love, Jesus brought us grace,
mercy and peace; and has called us,
in turn, to be creatures of peace
(cf. Mt 5:9), in mercy, in justice,
and in love.

**Hands of blood, ideologies of violence,
enemies of peace ...**
You, O God, came on earth
to teach us
to scorn every resentment which we cherish
in hearts that are violent
and without pity;
— when, oh when, will we sing a new song
of universal peace?

THE LORD IS LEADER

from Psalm 127

Unless Yahweh builds the house,
its builders work in vain.
Unless Yahweh guards the city,
the watchers guard in vain.

It is vain to rise early
and stay up late,
toiling for food;
Yahweh provides for the beloved
while they sleep.

Yahweh gives children as a gift,
the fruit of the womb, a blessing.
Like arrows in a warrior's hand
are the children of one's youth.

Blessed are those with quivers full of them;
they will not be dismayed,
fighting foes at the gate.

Without the goodness and inspiration of the Lord, we cannot succeed in building anything, whether it be in the family, in the community, in the church, in the world, in the working place. It is God who causes us to grow (cf. 1 Cor 3:7). In the acceptance of God's love, in the availability of God's will for us, in the striving to make that same love the basis of our relationships, will God's presence in us be alive and active (cf. Jn 15:9-17).

It is the Lord who builds
and keeps us alive;
every stone of the church
is a gift of God,
and the surplus —
of which there is plenty —
is of no use;
those who return to God
are a more living church,
— a more fervent one.

GOD GUIDES HISTORY

from Psalm 94

O Yahweh, the one you instruct is blessed,
the one you teach from your law,
to bring relief in troubled days.

Yahweh will not abandon
nor forsake God's chosen people;
verdicts will once more be founded on justice,
followed by all who are honest of heart.

Who fights for me against oppression?
Who stands at my side against injustice?
If Yahweh had not been my helper,
I would soon have lived in the silent grave.

When I said that my foot was slipping,
O Yahweh, your faithful love held me up.
When troubled thoughts filled my heart,
your comfort filled my soul with joy.

Do you support a corrupt court,
one that makes misery by its laws?
They band together against the just
and execute the innocent.

But Yahweh has been my strong tower,
my God, the rock where I can flee.

*'**I** am the Lord your God,*
who teaches you to profit,
who leads you in the way you
should go' (Is 48:17).
The truth, the light, the wisdom,
and the love of the Lord, change
our earthly travels into a marvellous
journey, even if people must cross
troubled waters (cf. Wis 10:17-18). It
is necessary, therefore to recognise and
follow the loving guidance of God.

If wickedness becomes the rule
and judges of this world
are masters of injustice,
I will wait for the winds to ease;
for then I would have no cause to be ashamed
of my humanity.
Meanwhile, whoever is alone,
hears the hissing sounds of death,
the cursing of the violent,
without being able to see.
While you, O God, watch and listen.
When will you shout and sweep away wind —
and cloud? hisses — and curses?
I hope you will do this, because — I love you
and I love still the mystery of my humanity.

THE TASTE OF LIBERTY

from Psalm 126

When Yahweh returned the exiles to Zion
we were like dreamers;

With mouths full of laughter,
tongues singing for joy.

Word passed round the nations,
'These are Yahweh's great deeds for them!'
Yes! Yahweh did great things for us,
and we are glad.

O Yahweh, bring our good fortune back,
like torrents in the south.
To sow in tears means joyful reaping.

Those who go forth weeping,
bearing the seed for sowing
return singing joyfully,
bearing the sheaves.

The Lord 'has sent me to proclaim release to captives and recovering of sight to the blind, to set at liberty those who are oppressed' (Lk 4:18). The same mission accomplished by Jesus is entrusted to us today and Jesus wants us all to continue, in time, the work of the redemption of humanity, so that each one of us can sing the joyful song of freedom.

I have repented —
there is peace in my heart
and I am free;
turning back to you, Lord,
takes me along a pathway of hope
as I quicken my step towards you.

THE FIRMNESS OF THE LOVE OF GOD

from Psalm 125

If you trust in Yahweh you are like Mount Zion:
it cannot be shaken,
it stands firm forever.
As the mountains encircle Jerusalem,
so the people are encircled by Yahweh,
both now and forever.

The rule of the wicked must not continue
over the heritage of the upright,
or the upright might turn
their own hands to evil.

Do good, O Yahweh, to those who are good,
the honest of heart.
But those who turn to wicked ways
are banished by Yahweh with evildoers.
May Israel have peace!

In the same way that Jesus walked before, and with, the disciples (cf. Mk 10:32), so now the same Jesus walks with us, actually helping us to walk if we are lame, or sick, or weak (cf. Mt 8:7). This goodness of Jesus gives us the courage and strength to go along the ways of the world in the company of the Spirit (cf. Rom 8:4).

I know you are within me, God,
and that is enough for me;
there is no storm
which can frighten me.